Vegan Budget cookbook

33 Delicious Low-Cost Vegan Recipes
Quick and Easy to Make

Green Protein

Table of Content

Introduction

Hi,

Thank you for downloading my book, *"Vegan Quick Meals"*. It is a complete cookbook for vegan recipes, and I hope you'll enjoy it. This book contains a brief introduction to vegan lifestyle along with 30+ delicious high protein recipes.

In the past 20 years, vegan lifestyle has gained huge popularity. Hundreds of books have been written on this topic. The vegan lifestyle is a way of living rather than a diet plan. Practice the vegan lifestyle and you'll understand its importance.

Vegan lifestyle offers many health benefits. The fiber consumption, unsaturated fats, magnesium, and essential minerals contribute to your heart health. There are many choices and creative ways to prepare vegan meals. You can choose green foods, raw vegetables, and fruits.

The vegan lifestyle has gained popularity, but people think that the vegan lifestyle costs **money** or **time**. I planned to prove them wrong.

I am a vegan myself. It is not easy to adopt a vegan lifestyle with a busy schedule. I do not want to skip a healthy meal, but I can't spend the entire day in the kitchen. I know this problem exists in every household.

I have been searching for some quick and delicious vegan recipes. After spending 20 weekends in research (cooking), I have put together these vegan recipes that I would like to share with you. In this book, I have listed 30+ recipes that are super affordable, tasty and easy to make. You can prepare most meals in just 30 minutes. Some can be cooked in less than 15 minutes.

Protein Issues with Vegan Diet

Vegan diets have low protein. Protein is the building block of our body. Lysine is the most important component of protein consumption. If you consume enough lysine, you can fulfill protein requirements. However, there is no system to create lysine in the body, although other amino acids can be created. Lysine must be obtained from some outside sources.

Legumes, seitan, soy meat and tofu provide a high number of lysine components. There are other legume foods and green veggies that provide essential protein components. You do not have to search for them. A complete list is presented in this book.

This book is also special in another way. It is a compilation of affordable vegan recipes. A vegan lifestyle is different than any other diet plan. It does not cost hundreds of dollars. You do not need any "new" ingredient or tool to prepare these recipes. All ingredients are easily available in the market for an affordable price.

Each recipe costs less than a coffee cup. I have divided these recipes into three sections:

1. Recipes that cost only 3$.

2. Recipes with a 5$ budget mark.

3. Nutritional recipes for only 7$ per meal.

Now you can prepare a meal in less than 30 minutes for 3$ only. Do not worry, it is not going to be a boring food item. You'll love the taste, cooking style, and vegan diet essentials. These recipes can be customized according to personal requirements. After a long, tedious day, just come home and try these recipes. Each tested recipe has a list of common ingredients. You can easily purchase them at the grocery store and store a bunch for the entire week. Each recipe has a list of steps with clear directions. Each step contributes to a tasty vegan recipe.

This book takes care of the nutritional information. Also, you are getting another advantage. These recipes help you lose weight. In fact, the vegan lifestyle is designed to maintain a healthy weight. You do not consume saturated fats. You consume fiber in a high amount. In short words, you get a complete, balanced diet plan. The only problem was a lack of protein, and it is fixed in this book.

Enough said. Let's get started and try these delicious vegan recipes.

Chapter 1: 3 Dollars Max

Fried Pineapple Rice

Total Preparation & Cooking time: 30 mins.

Servings: 6

Ingredients

- 1 chopped onion, small
- 2 tbsp. raisins
- 1 tbsp. sesame oil
- 2 to 3 cups brown rice, cooked & cooled
- 1/2 to 3/4 cup chopped pineapple
- 1 tbsp. soy sauce (or Braggs liquid amino)
- 1 tsp. curry powder
- 1/2 tsp. ground turmeric
- 1 chopped tomatoes, small
- 1/8 tsp. black pepper
- 2 tbsp. chopped cilantro, fresh
- 1/8 tsp. sea salt

Directions

1. On medium heat in a large saucepan heat the sesame oil & sauté the onions until translucent.

2.   Add the pineapple, cooked rice, Braggs, raisins, tomato, turmeric and curry powder.

3.   Mix thoroughly & cook until all of the ingredients are heated throughout approximately 8 to 10 minutes.

4.   Season with pepper and salt. Garnish with fresh cilantro. Serve & enjoy!

Nutritional Value (Amount Per Serving): 178.4 Calories, 4.4 g Total Fat, 0 mg Cholesterol, 32.6 g Total Carbohydrate, 3 g Dietary Fiber, 3 g Protein

Scrambled Tofu

Total Preparation & Cooking time: 25 mins

Servings: 6

Ingredients

- 1 pound of firm tofu
- 2 chopped green onions or 1 tbsp. onion powder
- 1 tbsp. soy sauce
- 1/4 tsp. turmeric
- 2 tbsp. green pimientos, dried (optional) or 1 tbsp. green chilies, canned (optional)
- 1 to 2 chopped tomatoes
- 1 chopped green bell pepper
- 1 tbsp. Italian seasoning
- 1/2 tsp. salt
- black salt, to taste

Directions

1. Use your hands to crumble the tofu.

2. Mix tofu and everything together in a skillet but don't mix the tomatoes. Heat approximately 5 to 10 minutes.

3. Now put in the tomatoes & then continue heating approximately 5 to 10 minutes more (until thoroughly heated).

Nutritional Value (Amount Per Serving): 66.7 Calories, 3.2 g Total Fat, 0 mg Cholesterol, 4.2 g Total Carbohydrate, 1.4 g Dietary Fiber, 7 g Protein

Lentil Quinoa Salad

Total Preparation & Cooking time: 35 mins

Servings: 4

Ingredients

- 2 chopped green onions (can substitute with red onion as well)
- 1/2 cup quinoa
- 1/2 cup lentils
- 1/4 cup canola oil
- 2 tbsp. red wine vinegar
- 1/4 tsp. garlic powder
- 1 tsp. Dijon mustard
- Zest of 1 lime
- 1 tbsp. cilantro, fresh & chopped
- 3 and 1/4 cups water
- black pepper and kosher salt

Directions

1. Rinse the quinoa in cold water and put it in a sieve. Add 1 and 1/4 cups of water and the rinsed quinoa in a microwave-proof bowl (preferably large and with a cover). Cover and heat on high settings approximately 10 minutes. Let the quinoa to sit approximately 2 minutes and then stir. Make sure that upon biting, Quinoa must be a little "pop", but tender enough to eat.

2. Now rinse the quinoa in cold water & put it in a sieve again. Simmer the lentils in two cups of water in a saucepan

approximately half an hour. Make sure that the lentils are not soft, but tender enough. Drain & cool.

3.   Whisk the vinegar and mustard together in a small bowl & drizzle in the oil to make a mixture. Put in the lime zest, garlic powder, and pepper, and salt, to taste.

4.   To bring the salad together: Mix the lentils, quinoa, chopped cilantro, and green onions in a salad bowl, preferably medium. Put the salad ingredients on the dressing, toss well to coat evenly and serve.

Nutritional Value (Amount Per Serving): 237.7 Calories, 15.1 g Total Fat, 0 mg Cholesterol, 21.2 g Total Carbohydrate, 4.2 g Dietary Fiber, 5.6 g Protein

Chickpea & Avocado Salad Sandwich

Total Preparation & Cooking time: 10 mins

Servings: 4

Ingredients

- 1 can garbanzo beans (15 oz.) or 1 can chickpeas (approximately 15 oz.)
- Juice of 1 lime
- 1/4 cup cilantro, fresh & chopped
- 1 ripe avocado, large
- 2 tbsp. green onions, chopped
- slices of whole wheat bread (or any of your choice)
- pepper and salt, to taste

Directions

1. Rinse the chickpeas using cold water and then drain. Place the chickpeas on a paper towel & get rid of the external skins.

2. Smash the avocado and chickpeas using a potato masher or fork together in a medium bowl. Add in green onion, cilantro & lime juice. Season with pepper and salt, to taste.

3. Spread salad on your favorite bread & top it with your desired sandwich toppings.

4. Try eating the sandwich the same day.

Nutritional Value (Amount Per Serving): 302.6 Calories, 13.4 g Total Fat, 0 mg Cholesterol, 40.5 g Total Carbohydrate, 11.8 g Dietary Fiber, 8.8 g Protein

Curried Lentils and Rice

Total Preparation & Cooking time: 50 mins.

Servings: 4

Ingredients

- 1 tart apple, large & diced
- 2 vegetable bouillon cubes
- 3 minced garlic cloves
- 1/2 chopped onion
- 2 to 3 tsp. curry powder, to taste
- 1 cup brown rice, washed
- 1/2 tsp. turmeric
- 1/4 tsp. ground ginger
- 4 cups water
- 3/4 cup lentils, dried
- 1/3 cup currants or 1/3 cup raisins
- 1 to 2 tbsp. vegetable broth
- salt

Directions

1. Heat the vegetable broth in a Dutch oven, saucepan, or soup pot (preferably heavy-bottomed) & sauté 1 clove of the garlic with the onion until it starts becoming translucent.

2. Add the curry powder, turmeric, and ginger & sauté approximately 3 to 4 minutes or more.

3. If required, add more quantity of broth, and then the rice and sauté approximately 2 to 3 minutes.

4. Add 4 cups of water, lentils, remaining garlic, raisins, and bouillon cubes & bring to a boil.

5. Cover and simmer approximately half an hour, on low heat.

6. Put the apples in and simmer. Cover until the water is completely absorbed, or for 10 to 15 minutes more.

7. You may also top with some more raisins and plain yogurt and serve.

Nutritional Value (Amount Per Serving): 376.7 Calories, 2.1 g Total Fat, 0 mg Cholesterol, 77.5 g Total Carbohydrate, 15.1 g Dietary Fiber, 13.9 g Protein

Spinach and Orange Salad

Total Preparation & Cooking time: 15 mins.

Servings: 6

Ingredients

* 3 oranges, medium peeled, seeded & sectioned
* 3/4-pound spinach fresh, bite-size pieces
* 1/4 to 1/3 cup French dressing
* 1 red onion, medium, sliced & separated into rings

Directions

1. Carefully wash the spinach using cold water and let it dry.

2. In a large salad bowl, mix the spinach, sliced onion, and orange sections together, toss to coat well.

3. Drizzle the dressing over the spinach mixture and toss smoothly.

Nutritional Value (Amount Per Serving): 98.8 Calories, 5 g Total Fat, 0 mg Cholesterol, 13.1 g Total Carbohydrate, 3.1 g Dietary Fiber, 2.5 g Protein

Confetti Orzo Salad

Total Preparation & Cooking time: 20 mins.

Servings: 6

Ingredients

- 1 carrot, finely diced
- 1 and a 1/2 cups orzo pasta
- 1/8 tsp. black pepper
- 1/2 tsp. lemon zest
- 1/4 cup diced red onion, (approximately half onion, small)
- 1 minced garlic clove
- 1 1/4 cups bell peppers (green, red & yellow)
- 1/3 cup olive oil
- 3 tbsp. lemon juice
- 1/4 cup finely chopped parsley, fresh
- 1/2 tsp. salt

Directions

1. Use a lot of boiling water to cook the orzo until tender, approximately 10 to 12 minutes and then let it drain.

2. Whisk lemon juice, oil, salt, zest, garlic, and pepper until well blended.

3. Toss everything together. You may either serve it hot or cold.

Nutritional Value (Amount Per Serving): 417.5 Calories, 19.1 g Total Fat, 0 mg Cholesterol, 53 g Total Carbohydrate, 3.6 g Dietary Fiber, 9.1 g Protein

Sweet Potato and Lentil Soup

Total Preparation & Cooking time: 40 mins.

Servings: 6

Ingredients

- 1 cup red lentil
- 750 grams' sweet potatoes
- 3 onions, medium
- 1/4 tsp. cayenne
- 1 lemon
- 5 garlic cloves
- 1/2 tsp. ground turmeric
- 2 tsp. ground cumin
- 1/2 cup chopped coriander
- 5 cups water
- black pepper and salt

Directions

1. Peel & roughly chop the sweet potatoes and onions - can be little thick.

2. Combine the lentils, garlic, water, cumin, turmeric and cayenne together in a medium pot.

3. Cover; bring to the boil. Simmer approximately half an hour, until the lentils and potatoes are completely cooked.

4. Puree the soup, adding the lemon juice and the coriander. Add pepper and salt to taste.

Nutritional Value (Amount Per Serving): 322.2 Calories, 3.4 g Total Fat, 6 mg Cholesterol, 58.5 g Total Carbohydrate, 8.6 g Dietary Fiber, 16 g Protein

Chapter 2: 5 Dollars Max

Potato and Kale Soup

Total Preparation & Cooking time: 55 mins.

Servings: 3

Ingredients

- 1/2 pound trimmed & shredded kale
- 3 peeled & sliced potatoes
- 1 chopped onion, medium
- 3 minced cloves garlic
- 4 tsp. olive oil
- 4 cups water
- 1/4 tsp. black pepper

Directions

1. Cook onion in oil in a pan (preferably large), until tender.

2. Mix in potatoes, water, and garlic; bring to a boil approximately 5 minutes; decrease the heat & continue cooking until potatoes are tender or for 20 more minutes or so.

3. Mash the potatoes in the liquid; mix in the pepper and kale; simmer till kale is done approximately 15 minutes, then serve.

Nutritional Value (Amount Per Serving): 411.9 Calories, 10.2 g Total Fat, 0 mg Cholesterol, 74 g Total Carbohydrate, 10.4 g Dietary Fiber, 11.1 g Protein

Spicy Black Bean Burgers

Total Preparation & Cooking time: 25 mins.

Servings: 6

Ingredients

- 1 minced jalapeno pepper, small
- 1⁄2 cup flour
- 2 minced garlic cloves
- 1⁄2 tsp. oregano, dried
- 1 diced onion, small
- 1⁄2 cup corn nib lets
- 2 cups mashed black beans, canned
- 1⁄4 cup breadcrumbs
- 2 tsp. minced parsley (optional)
- 1⁄4 tsp. cumin
- 1 tbsp. olive oil
- 1⁄2 diced red pepper, medium
- 2 tsp. chili powder
- 1⁄2 tsp. salt

Directions

1. To coat, set aside the flour on a small plate. Sauté the garlic, onion, hot peppers, and oregano in oil on medium-high heat settings in a medium saucepan, until the onions are translucent. Put in the peppers & sauté until pepper is tender, approximately 2 more minutes. Keep it aside.

2.	Use a fork or potato masher to mash the black beans in a large bowl. Stir in the vegetables cumin, breadcrumbs, chili powder, parsley and salt. Mix well and divide to make 6 patties.

3.	Coat each side of the patty by laying it down in the flour. Cook the patties on a lightly oiled frying pan until browned on either sides or approximately 10 minutes on medium-high heat.

Nutritional Value (Amount Per Serving): 172.4 Calories, 3.2 g Total Fat, 0 mg Cholesterol, 29.7 g Total Carbohydrate, 7.1 g Dietary Fiber, 7.3 g Protein

Chinese Cabbage & Parsley Salad

Total Preparation & Cooking time: 20 mins.

Servings: 4

Ingredients

- 1 cup carrot, shredded
- 1 cup pineapple, chopped (juice reserved, drained)
- 4 cups shredded Chinese cabbage,
- 4 tbsp. pineapple juice, reserved
- 2 cups roughly chopped parsley, fresh
- 1/4 cup mayonnaise
- 1 tbsp. grated ginger
- 1/2 thinly sliced red onion,
- 1 tbsp. whole grain mustard
- black pepper, freshly ground & salt to taste

Directions

1. Combine pineapple, parsley, cabbage, thinly sliced red onion and shredded carrot in a large zip-lock bag; seal & let it chill.

2. Combine whole grain mustard, mayonnaise, pineapple, juice ginger, freshly ground black pepper and salt to taste; cover & chill.

3. Put the dressing mixture in the zip-lock bag mixture and toss to coat well, just before serving.

4. Serve and enjoy!

Nutritional Value (Amount Per Serving): 77.2 Calories, 0.8 g Total Fat, 0 mg Cholesterol, 17.2 g Total Carbohydrate, 4 g Dietary Fiber, 2.8 g Protein

Spice Roasted Butternut Squash

Total Preparation & Cooking time: 45 mins.

Servings: 4

Ingredients

- 1 butternut squash, (approximately 850 grams)
- 1 tsp. ground coriander
- 1 tsp. cumin seed
- 2 tbsp. olive oil
- 1 tsp. red pepper flakes, crushed
- 1/2 tsp. sea salt

Directions

1. Preheat your oven to 200 C/ 392F.

2. Peel the butternut squash and then divide it in two lengthwise. Scoop out and get rid of the seeds.

3. Cube the flesh.

4. In a roasting tin, put the olive oil & then place the tine in the oven.

5. Place the chili, cumin, salt and coriander in a pestle & mortar. Crush simultaneously.

6. Chuck the flavors into the hot oil and then put in the butternut squash, toss well. Make sure that the pieces are well coated in the spiced oil.

7. Roast until the butternut squash becomes golden brown and tender, approximately half an hour, turning now and then.

Nutritional Value (Amount Per Serving): 159.2 Calories, 7.2 g Total Fat, 0 mg Cholesterol, 25.5 g Total Carbohydrate, 4.6 g Dietary Fiber, 2.3 g Protein

Chickpea Snacks

Total Preparation & Cooking time: 40 mins.

Servings: 1 Cup

Ingredients

- 1 and 1/2 tsp. chili powder
- 1 tsp. paprika
- 1/2 tsp. oregano
- 1 can chickpeas, drained (approximately 15 oz.)
- 1 tsp. corn flour
- 1/3 tsp. onion powder or 1/3 tsp. garlic powder
- 1 dash cayenne pepper
- 1/3 tsp. Cilantro, ground
- 1/2 tsp. cumin
- 1 tbsp. vegetable oil

For cheesy flavor:

- 1 to 2 tsp. nutritional yeast
- Salt

Directions

1. Preheat your oven at 190C /375F.

2. Mix oil and chickpeas in a small bowl.

3. Mix spices & corn flour together in a small ball (don't add the salt). Now put in the chickpeas & toss to coat well.

4. Bake on a baking sheet until crunchy approximately half an hour (or little more).

5. Sprinkle salt over the chickpeas.

Nutritional Value (Amount Per Serving): 674.2 Calories, 20 g Total Fat, 0 mg Cholesterol, 104.3 g Total Carbohydrate, 22.5 g Dietary Fiber, 24.1 g Protein

Red Lentil Soup

Total Preparation & Cooking time: 50 mins.

Servings: 4

Ingredients

- 1 cup lentil, red, washed & cleaned
- 1/4 cup finely chopped mild onion
- 4 cups of vegetable stock
- 1 tsp. paprika
- 1/2 cup peeled & diced white potato
- pepper (to taste)
- 1 tsp. salt (to taste)

Directions

1. Arrange the lentils in a colander & rinse using cold water.

2. Search for the damaged beans and remove them.

3. In a medium pot, put the red lentils with the potatoes, stock, paprika and onions.

4. Bring the pot to a boil & decrease the heat to simmer.

5. Place a lid loosely on the pot and leave it slightly open to allow the evaporation process.

6. Cook until the lentils are tender, approximately half an hour.

7. Add pepper and salt to taste.

8. Place 1 cup of the soup either into a food processor or blender and blend for a short time.

9. Put the blended soup back to the pot with the cup of soup held in reserve.

10. Heat through & serve hot.

Nutritional Value (Amount Per Serving): 188.2 Calories, 1.2 g Total Fat, 0 mg Cholesterol, 33.6 g Total Carbohydrate, 5.9 g Dietary Fiber, 12.5 g Protein

Totally Vegetable Soup

Total Preparation & Cooking time: 35 mins.

Servings: 4

Ingredients

- 3 cups broth, fat free
- 2 minced cloves garlic
- 2/3 cup carrot, sliced
- 1/2 cup beans, green
- 1 and 1/2 cups green cabbage, diced
- 1/2 tsp. basil, dried
- 1 tbsp. tomato paste
- 1/4 tsp. oregano, dried
- 1/2 cup onion, diced
- 1/2 cup zucchini, diced
- 1/4 tsp. salt

Directions

1. Use cooking spray and spray a non-sticking saucepan (preferably large).

2. Sauté the garlic, carrot and onion over low heat approximately 5 minutes, until softened.

3. Add cabbage, broth, tomato paste, green beans and simmer, covered until beans are tender, approximately 15 minutes.

4.   Stir in the zucchini & heat approximately five more minutes.

5.   Serve hot.

Nutritional Value (Amount Per Serving): 42.2 Calories, 0.4 g Total Fat, 0.3 mg Cholesterol, 8.8 g Total Carbohydrate, 2.3 g Dietary Fiber, 1.9 g Protein

Oven-Roasted Asparagus

Total Preparation & Cooking time: 12 mins.

Servings: 4

Ingredients

- 1/4 cup parmesan cheese, course grated
- 1 and 1/2 pounds' asparagus, tough stems removed & washed
- 1/2 tsp. Italian seasoning
- 3 tbsp. balsamic vinegar
- 1 tbsp. olive oil, lite
- pepper and salt

Directions

1. In a hot oven, heat an Oven proof pan (preferably 10") approximately 5 minutes.

2. Add the olive oil & then the Italian seasoning to the pan.

3. Coat the pan entirely.

4. To coat all sides of the asparagus, roll it in the oil.

5. Bake in 200C/400F oven approximately 7 to 8 minutes, don't overcook. Ensure that the asparagus is very crisp & heated through completely.

6. Remove from the oven and drizzle the vinegar.

7.   Add pepper & salt.

8.   Sprinkle Parmesan cheese on the asparagus.

9.   Serve at room temperature or serve hot.

Nutritional Value (Amount Per Serving):77.8 Calories, 3.8 g Total Fat, 0 mg Cholesterol, 9 g Total Carbohydrate, 3.4 g Dietary Fiber, 4.1 g Protein

Fried Tofu

Total Preparation & Cooking time: 20 mins.

Servings: 3

Ingredients

- 1/4 cup nutritional yeast, Red Star
- 3 tbsp. soya sauce or 3 tbsp. tamari
- 1 tsp. seasoning
- 1 package tofu, extra firm (approximately 350 g)
- 1 tbsp. olive oil

Directions

1. Use olive oil to grease a pan lightly (preferably non-sticking).

2. Put soy sauce (tamari) in a bowl.

3. Mix spices and yeast in a different bowl.

4. Slice the tofu into slices, preferably ¼".

5. Dip the tofu in the soy sauce and then in yeast mixture.

6. Fry approximately 2 to 3 minutes, until golden; flip & brown the other side as well.

7. If required, add a bit of oil.

Nutritional Value (Amount Per Serving): 198.4 Calories, 14.1 g Total Fat, 0 mg Cholesterol, 4.5 g Total Carbohydrate, 1.8 g Dietary Fiber, 17.2 g Protein

Roasted Brussels Sprouts

Total Preparation & Cooking time: 30 mins.

Servings: 4

Ingredients

- 1 and 1/2 pounds Brussels sprouts, fresh
- 3 tbsp. olive oil, extra virgin
- 1/2 tsp. garlic powder
- 1/2 tsp. black pepper, ground
- 1/2 tsp. salt
- 1/2 tsp. Sage, dried

Directions

1. Preheat your oven to 200C/400 F.

2. Cut off each Brussels sprouts bottom (roughly 1/4") and then slice them in half lengthwise.

3. Toss everything together and then put the mixture on a baking dish, in a single layer.

4. Roast until Brussels sprouts are tender throughout and slightly browned, approximately half an hour.

5. Serve hot or at room temperature

Nutritional Value (Amount Per Serving): 165 Calories, 10.7 g Total Fat, 0 mg Cholesterol, 15.8 g Total Carbohydrate, 6.6 g Dietary Fiber, 5.9 g Protein

Pinto Bean, Fresh Corn and Tomato Salad

Total Preparation & Cooking time: 30 mins.

Servings: 4

Ingredients

For Dressing

- 2 tbsp. Italian parsley, fresh & chopped
- 2 tbsp. olive oil, extra virgin
- 2 minced cloves garlic
- 2 tbsp. lemon juice, fresh

For Salad

- 1 can pinto beans rinsed & drained (16 oz.)
- 7 or 8 ears fresh corn (approximately 2 cups)
- 1 cup plum tomato, seeded & chopped
- 1/4 cup basil, fresh & chopped
- 1/2 cup Vidalia onion or 1/2 cup red onions, chopped

Directions

1. Chop the basil, onion and tomatoes, wash & drain the pinto beans as well.

2. Grill the fresh corn on the outdoor/indoor grill or barbeque until done.

3. Cut off the kernels into a bowl.

4. Combine the pinto beans, the corn kernels, basil, onion, and tomatoes in the same large bowl.

5. Whisk lemon juice, olive oil, garlic and parsley to blend in a separate small bowl.

6. Transfer the dressing on the corn mixture & stir to combine.

7. Season with pepper and salt and serve at room temperature.

Nutritional Value (Amount Per Serving): 307.6 Calories, 8.6 g Total Fat, 0 mg Cholesterol, 48.9 g Total Carbohydrate, 13.2 g Dietary Fiber, 13.5 g Protein

Spicy Thai Peanut Noodles

Total Preparation & Cooking time: 30 mins.

Servings: 4

Ingredients

- 6 mushrooms, sliced
- 3 tbsp. soy sauce
- 1/2 cup vegetable stock
- 8 oz. spaghetti
- 2 to 3 tbsp. peanut butter, natural-style
- 1 and 1/2 tbsp. ginger (fresh & minced)
- 2 tbsp. honey
- 1 tsp. ground coriander
- 2 tsp. ground cumin
- 1 tsp. red pepper flakes
- 3 to 4 minced garlic cloves
- 1 cup small broccoli floret
- 1/2 chopped green pepper
- 1 julienned carrot

Directions

1. Cook 8oz of pasta as per the directions (linguine or spaghetti). When done, keep it aside.

2. Sauté the veggies of your choice in a pan with a small quantity of oil, until cooked. Keep it aside.

3. In a small sauce pan, stir soy sauce, vegetable stock, honey, peanut butter, cumin, ginger, coriander, garlic and red pepper flakes together.

4. Cook over medium heat settings until sauce is heated through & honey and peanut butter melts.

5. Add fried veggies, noodles in the pan stir; toss to coat well.

Nutritional Value (Amount Per Serving): 440.7 Calories, 7.4 g Total Fat, 0 mg Cholesterol, 79.5 g Total Carbohydrate, 5.2 g Dietary Fiber, 17.3 g Protein

Quinoa Stir Fry with Spinach & Walnuts

Total Preparation & Cooking time: 40 mins.

Servings: 4

Ingredients

* 1 cup cherry tomatoes or 1 cup grape tomatoes
* 1/2 cup grated cheese, Parmigiano-Reggiano
* 2 tbsp. olive oil, extra virgin
* 1 cup quinoa
* 1/2 cup walnut pieces
* 1/2 tsp. garlic clove, minced
* baby spinach leaves
* basil leaf, fresh

Directions

1. Add plenty of water in a small bowl so that it covers the quinoa properly and swish to rinse. Transfer the quinoa into a mesh strainer & drain well.

2. In medium skillet, heat oil over medium heat and add the quinoa. Stir and toast over medium heat settings approximately 10 minutes, until golden. Add garlic & cook for an additional minute. Add 2 cups of water and salt and bring to boil. Cover; cook over medium-low heat approximately 15 to 20 minutes, until water is absorbed.

3. In a small skillet, spread the walnuts & stir over medium-low heat approximately 5 minutes, until well toasted. Keep it aside.

4. Add tomatoes and spinach to the skillet; when quinoa is cooked. Stir fry over medium heat approximately a minute or two, until tomatoes are warm and spinach is nearly wilted. Stir in cheese and walnuts and garnish with basil. Serve hot.

Nutritional Value (Amount Per Serving): 360.4 Calories, 21.7 g Total Fat, 7.2 mg Cholesterol, 31.2 g Total Carbohydrate, 4.4 g Dietary Fiber, 12.4 g Protein

Roasted Parmesan Garlic Cauliflower

Total Preparation & Cooking time: 45 mins.

Servings: 6

Ingredients

- 3 tbsp. garlic, fresh & minced
- 1/3 cup parmesan cheese, grated
- 1 head cauliflower, separated in florets
- parsley, chopped & fresh
- 3 tbsp. olive oil
- black pepper and salt, to taste

Directions

1. Preheat your oven to 230 C/ 450 F and grease a casserole dish, preferably large.

2. In large re-sealable bag, put garlic olive oil and cauliflower. Shake well so that it gets mixed completely.

3. Transfer the ingredients into already prepared casserole dish.

4. Bake approximately half an hour, stirring halfway through.

5. Top with parsley and Parmesan and broil until golden brown, approximately 3 to 5 minutes.

Nutritional Value (Amount Per Serving): 114.3 Calories, 8.6 g Total Fat, 4.9 mg Cholesterol, 6.5 g Total Carbohydrate, 2 g Dietary Fiber, 4.3 g Protein

Chapter 3: 7 Dollars Max

Vegetable and Tofu with Peanut Sauce

Total Preparation & Cooking time: 30 mins.

Servings: 4

Ingredients

- 1/3 cup roasted peanuts, dry & chopped
- 8 oz. whole wheat spaghetti, uncooked
- 1 and 1/2 tbsp. soy sauce, low sodium
- 3 tbsp. creamy peanut butter
- 1/4 tsp. red pepper flakes, crushed or 1/4 tsp. hot chili sauce
- 1 tsp. garlic, minced
- 1/4 cup teriyaki sauce, low-sodium
- 2 tbsp. hot water
- 1 bag frozen vegetables (approximately 16 oz. stir fry variety)
- 2 tbsp. soy sauce or 2 tbsp. teriyaki sauce
- 1 extra firm tofu, water-packed (approximately 16 oz. & drained)
- 2 tsp. sesame oil

Directions

1. Place tofu among a number of paper towels layers (preferably heavy-duty) and prepare the tofu. Cover tofu with some more paper towels, pressing occasionally and let the tofu stand approximately 5 minutes.

2. Cut the tofu into ½" cubes and then place the tofu in a bowl. Add either teriyaki sauce or soy sauce, and toss well to coat the tofu completely. Cover; chill for a minimum period of an hour.

3. Cook the pasta according to directions mentioned on the package, omitting fat and salt; drain and keep it aside.

4. Combine hot water, teriyaki sauce, red pepper flakes (or hot Chile sauce), and peanut butter, stirring with a whisk.

5. Over medium-high heat in a large nonstick skillet, heat the sesame oil. Add the minced garlic and sauté approximately a minute.

6. Add the tofu with the pasta and sauté until tofu has browned a little, approximately 5 minutes.

7. Add the teriyaki sauce mixture & cook approximately 2 to 3 minutes.

8. Add soy sauce, vegetables, and pasta; cook until heated thoroughly, stirring well.

9. Remove the pasta from the heat & sprinkle peanuts over it.

Nutritional Value (Amount Per Serving): 553.6 Calories, 23.3 g Total Fat, 0 mg Cholesterol, 68.7 g Total Carbohydrate, 7.1 g Dietary Fiber, 27.9 g Protein

African Vegetable Soup

Total Preparation & Cooking time: 50 mins.

Servings: 6

Ingredients

- 1 cup chickpeas (cooked or canned)
- 3 tbsp. vegetable oil
- 1 cup finely chopped onion
- 2 diced celery ribs
- 1 potato, small & chopped
- 1/8 tsp. cayenne
- 4 tomatoes, small & chopped
- 1 carrot, small & diced
- 4 cups vegetable stock
- 1 tsp. ground coriander
- 1/2 tsp. cinnamon
- 1 cup tomato juice
- 1 finely chopped zucchini, small
- 1/2 cup crumbled curly vermicelli
- 1 tsp. turmeric
- 1/4 cup lemon juice, fresh
- pepper and salt, to taste

Directions

1. Sauté the celery and onions in oil in a soup pot, until onions are translucent.

2. Add the potatoes, carrots, and spices. Cook for additional 5 minutes, stirring over and over again.

3. Mix in the tomato juice, tomatoes and stock. Simmer until the vegetables are just about tender.

4. Add the vermicelli and zucchini and simmer approximately 5 more minutes.

5. Mix in the lemon juice, chick peas, pepper and salt.

6. Garnish with mint leaves, chopped parsley, and strips of pimiento or red bell pepper.

Nutritional Value (Amount Per Serving): 172.3 Calories, 7.6 g Total Fat, 0 mg Cholesterol, 24.1 g Total Carbohydrate, 4.7 g Dietary Fiber, 4.2 g Protein

Ginger Peanut Soup

Total Preparation & Cooking time: 30 mins.

Servings: 6

Ingredients

- 1 and 1/2 cups chopped cauliflower
- 3 cups water or 3 cups vegetable stock
- 1 and 1/2 cups chopped broccoli
- 3 chopped cloves garlic
- 1 chopped onion, medium
- 5 tbsp. peanut butter, natural-style
- 1 tbsp. ginger, fresh & grated
- 1/4 tsp. cayenne pepper
- 1 can tomatoes, diced (approximately 28 oz.)
- 1/2 tsp. pepper
- 2 tbsp. olive oil
- 1/2 tsp. salt

Directions

1. On medium heat in a large soup pot, sauté the cauliflower, garlic, broccoli, ginger, onions, cayenne, pepper, and salt in oil until all of the vegetables are tender.

2. Add the peanut butter, stock, and tomatoes.

3. Decrease the heat & simmer approximately 20 to 22 minutes, stirring occasionally.

Nutritional Value (Amount Per Serving): 251.3 Calories, 17.5 g Total Fat, 0 mg Cholesterol, 19.7 g Total Carbohydrate, 5.9 g Dietary Fiber, 9 g Protein

African Pineapple Peanut Stew

Total Preparation & Cooking time: 30 mins.

Servings: 4

Ingredients

- 4 cups sliced kale
- 1 cup chopped onion
- 1/2 cup peanut butter
- 1 tbsp. hot pepper sauce or 1 tbsp. Tabasco sauce
- 2 minced garlic cloves
- 1/2 cup chopped cilantro
- 2 cups pineapple, undrained, canned & crushed
- 1 tbsp. vegetable oil

Directions

1. In a saucepan (preferably covered), sauté the garlic and onions in the oil until the onions are lightly browned, approximately 10 minutes, stirring often.

2. Wash the kale, till the time the onions are sauté.

3. Get rid of the stems. Mound the leaves on a cutting surface & slice crosswise into slices (preferably 1" thick).

4. Now put the pineapple and juice to the onions & bring to a simmer. Stir the kale in, cover and simmer until just tender, stirring frequently, approximately 5 minutes.

5. Mix in the hot pepper sauce, peanut butter & simmer for more 5 minutes.

6. Add salt according to your taste.

Nutritional Value (Amount Per Serving): 382 Calories, 20.3 g Total Fat, 0 mg Cholesterol, 27.6 g Total Carbohydrate, 5 g Dietary Fiber, 11.4 g Protein

Black Bean & Corn Salad with Avocado

Total Preparation & Cooking time: 20 mins.

Servings: 6

Ingredients

- 1 and 1/2 cups corn kernels, cooked & frozen or canned
- 1/2 cup olive oil
- 1 minced clove garlic
- 1/3 cup lime juice, fresh
- 1 avocado (peeled, pitted & diced)
- 1/8 tsp. cayenne pepper
- 2 cans black beans, (approximately 15 oz.)
- 6 thinly sliced green onions
- 1/2 cup chopped cilantro, fresh
- 2 chopped tomatoes
- 1 chopped red bell pepper
- chili powder
- 1/2 tsp. salt

Directions

1. In a small jar, place the olive oil, lime juice, garlic, cayenne, and salt.

2. Cover with lid; shake until all the ingredients under the jar are mixed well.

3. Toss the green onions, corn, beans, bell pepper, avocado, tomatoes, and cilantro together in a large bowl or plastic container with a cover.

4. Shake the lime dressing for a second time and transfer it over the salad ingredients.

5. Stir salad to coat the beans and vegetables with the dressing; cover & refrigerate.

6. To blend the flavors completely, let this sit a moment or two.

7. Remove the container from the refrigerator from time to time; turn upside down & back gently a couple of times to reorganize the dressing.

Nutritional Value (Amount Per Serving): 448 Calories, 24.3 g Total Fat, 0 mg Cholesterol, 50.8 g Total Carbohydrate, 14.3 g Dietary Fiber, 13.2 g Protein

Black Bean and Avocado Soup

Total Preparation & Cooking time: 35 mins.

Servings: 6

Ingredients

- 1 to 2 tsp. ground cumin
- 1⁄4 tsp. ground cinnamon
- 5 garlic cloves, minced
- 1 cup cheddar cheese, shredded
- 1⁄2 tsp. cayenne powder (to taste)
- 1 tsp. sugar
- 1⁄4 to 1⁄2 tsp. salt
- 3 cans black beans, drained (15 oz.)
- 1 red onion, diced
- 1⁄2 cup cilantro, fresh & chopped
- 6 plum tomatoes, seeded & coarsely chopped
- 2 Hass avocadoes (peeled, pitted & diced)
- 3 to 4 cups vegetable broth
- juice of fresh lime
- 2 tbsp. olive oil

Directions

1. Sauté garlic and onion in olive oil in a large soup pot until soft, approximately 7 to 10 minutes.

2.   Add cayenne powder, cumin, cinnamon, sugar, cilantro and salt; sauté until very fragrant, for 2 to 3 more minutes, stirring over and over again.

3.   Add beans and tomatoes; cook for 2 to 3 more minutes.

4.   Now put the broth in the pot & bring to a boil; approximately 15 to 20 minutes, simmer gently.

5.   Puree 1 cup of this mixture & return back to the pot.

6.   Stir in lime juice, and avocado. Heat through.

7.   Place in serving bowls & sprinkle with cheese.

Nutritional Value (Amount Per Serving): 443.9 Calories, 20.7 g Total Fat, 19.8 mg Cholesterol, 48.3 g Total Carbohydrate, 18.5 g Dietary Fiber, 20.4 g Protein

Vegan Nacho Cheese Sauce

Total Preparation & Cooking time: 30 mins.

Servings: 20

Ingredients

- 3 1/2 cups water
- juice of 2 lemons
- 2 cups cashews, raw
- 1 tsp. garlic powder
- 3/4 tsp. paprika
- 1 tsp. onion powder
- 1/2 cup nutritional yeast
- 1 can pimientos (7 oz. and include the liquid)
- 3 tsp. salt

Directions

1. Soak the raw cashews for couple of hours.

2. Put all of the ingredients with 2 and 1/2 cups of water into a blender & blend until smooth.

3. Transfer the blended mixture to a saucepan & add the left over water.

4. In a saucepan, heat the mixture approximately 20 minutes.

5. To prevent it from burning, stir continually.

6. If required, put more quantity of water to your desired consistency.

7. Use as a replacement for cheese or as a nacho cheese dip!

Nutritional Value (Amount Per Serving):98.8 Calories, 6.8 g Total Fat, 0 mg Cholesterol, 7.6 g Total Carbohydrate, 2 g Dietary Fiber, 4.2g Protein

Raw Vegan Chocolate Fruit Balls

Total Preparation & Cooking time: 5 mins.

Servings: 20 balls

Ingredients

- 1/2 cup raisins
- 1 cup nuts raw cashews, almonds, macadamias
- 2 tbsp. cocoa powder, unsweetened
- 1/2 cup apricot, dried & chopped
- 1 tbsp. orange juice, fresh
- 1/2 cup organic dates, pitted & chopped
- 2 drops of natural almond essence
- 1/4 cup coconut, desiccated
- 1/2 tsp. cinnamon

Directions

1. In a small bowl, mix the cinnamon and coconut together and keep it aside for rolling.

2. In a food processor, put all of the other ingredients, and if it doesn't get combined together completely, add in the orange juice slowly.

3. Make small balls from the mixture & coat the balls with coconut mixture.

4. Store in a refrigerator in an airtight glass container.

Nutritional Value (Amount Per Serving): 104 Calories, 5.8 g Total Fat, 0 mg Cholesterol, 12.7 g Total Carbohydrate, 2.3 g Dietary Fiber, 2.8 g Protein

Chapter 4: Affordable Guarantee

Macaroni and Yeast

Total Preparation & Cooking time: 40 mins.

Servings: 6

Ingredients

- 16 oz. vegan mayonnaise
- milk substitute, non-dairy
- 16 oz. elbow macaroni, small
- breadcrumbs
- 3 cups nutritional yeast
- pepper and salt

Directions

1. Preheat your oven to 350F/175C.

2. Make the noodles as per the directions mentioned on the package and then drain.

3. Add the ingredients in following orders now: jar of Vegenaise, yeast, pepper and salt.

4. While adding the milk substitute, stir well until creamy.

5. Pour the ingredients to the baking dish.

6. Sprinkle bread crumbs over the top.

7. Bake uncovered until golden brown, approximately half an hour.

Nutritional Value (Amount Per Serving): 847.7 Calories, 8.4 g Total Fat, 0 mg Cholesterol, 140.1 g Total Carbohydrate, 33.9 g Dietary Fiber, 70 g Protein

Oven Fries

Total Preparation & Cooking time: 50 mins.

Servings: 6

Ingredients

- 1 tsp. oregano, dried
- 2 tbsp. lemon juice
- 1 and 1/2 lbs. baking potatoes, unpeeled (approximately 3 medium)
- 1/4 tsp. pepper
- vegetable oil cooking spray
- 2 minced cloves garlic
- 2 tsp. olive oil
- 1/4 tsp. salt

Directions

1. Cut every potato into 8 wedges lengthwise.

2. In a large bowl, mix together the olive oil, lemon juice, pepper, oregano, garlic, and salt.

3. Add potatoes & toss to coat the ingredients well.

4. Place the potatoes on a baking sheet (skin side down) that is already coated with the cooking spray.

5. Bake at 400 F/200C until potatoes are lightly browned and tender, approximately 45 minutes.

Nutritional Value (Amount Per Serving):75.4 Calories, 1.6 g Total Fat, 0 mg Cholesterol, 14.5 g Total Carbohydrate, 1.3 g Dietary Fiber, 1.4 g Protein

Chilean Salad

Total Preparation & Cooking time: 5 mins.

Servings: 6

Ingredients

- 1 cup red onion or 1 cup sweet onions, finely sliced
- 3 cups tomatoes, sliced
- 1 tsp. lemon juice
- black pepper, freshly ground & salt
- 1 tbsp. coriander leaves, chopped
- 3 tbsp. olive oil

Directions

1   On a platter, mix together the onion, tomatoes, pepper and salt.

2   Combine lemon juice and oil and then transfer the mixture over the salad.

3   Sprinkle coriander leaves on the top.

Nutritional Value (Amount Per Serving): 86.7 Calories, 7 g Total Fat, 0 mg Cholesterol, 6 g Total Carbohydrate, 1.5 g Dietary Fiber, 1.1 g Protein

Glazed Mushrooms

Total Preparation & Cooking time: 15 mins.

Servings: 8

Ingredients

- 1-pound mushroom cap
- 2 tsp. basil
- 1 chopped green onion
- tbsp. olive oil
- 1 tbsp. chopped dill weed, fresh
- 1/2 tsp. paprika
- 3 tbsp. chopped parsley, fresh
- 1 crushed garlic clove
- 1/2 tsp. salt

Directions

1 Remove the stems from the mushrooms.

2 Over medium heat in a large non-stick skillet, heat the oil. Stir in garlic, green onion, paprika, and salt.

3 Increase the heat settings and add the mushrooms, sauté until mushrooms are well coated and glazed, approximately 3 to 5 minutes.

4 Remove the mushrooms from the heat. Toss in basil, dill and parsley.

5   Serve immediately.

Nutritional Value (Amount Per Serving): 59.4 Calories, 5.3 g
Total Fat, 0 mg Cholesterol, 2.3 g Total Carbohydrate, 0.7 g
Dietary Fiber, 1.9 g Protein

Conclusion

Thank you for downloading this book!

I hope this book can help you better plan your everyday meal and enjoy your Vegan lifestyle.

Finally, if you enjoyed this book, then I'd like to ask you for a favor, would you be kind enough to leave a review for this book on Amazon? It'd be greatly appreciated! Even if you think this book can use some improvements please let me know and I will take action upon it.

http://amzn.to/20KCx4l

Thank you and Happy Eating

Vegan Life Easy

High Protein Cookbook, Vegan Diet, Gluten Free & Dairy Free Recipes

Green Protein

Introduction

A person's health is considered to be the greatest wealth for a human being. "No" is a complete sentence and if you don't find the Healthy Foods passageway soon in your life, you will surely be discovering and experiencing sickness in your life.

Can you prevent your body from heart disease, overweight, diabetes, and some types of cancer?

If your answer is a "NO", then you've surely picked a right book.

This is not just another diet book. As you go through this book, you'll realize why you don't need to be an exercise "freak" in order to help prevent your body from contracting heart disease, overweight, diabetes, and some types of cancer and feel good.

What you need is to take charge of what you eat and when you eat. It's just that simple and pretty soon, you will notice a considerable change in your body, your energy levels, and your life.

A gluten-free, vegan diet is delicious and doable and you can prepare it in a very short span of time. When we say yes to health, we say no to harm.

Foods that come from animals including eggs and dairy products are not included under the "Vegan diet". Vegan diet only contains plants like grains, vegetables, fruits, nuts

& foods that you can prepare from the plants. Your body requires vitamins, minerals and trace elements as they are needed for your overall health, performance and physical wellbeing. In general, you would get them from a balanced vegan diet.

If you are interested in experiencing a healthier way of eating while avoiding the health risks that may result from unnecessary consumption of dairy, meat, and processed foods, then we suggest that you make the following foods the core of your diet:

A healthy vegan diet contains:

A lot of starchy food

A lot of vegetables and fruits

Few dairy alternatives like soya drinks, fortified

A small quantity of sugary and fatty foods

Some non-dairy protein sources, such as pulses and beans

Vegan diet would even help you to lose your added body weight:

Carbohydrate-rich food helps with permanent weight control as they contain less than half the calories of fat, which means that replacing fatty foods with compound carbs automatically cuts calories.

Both short-term and long-term, the most successful weight loss normally comes from keeping yourself away from animal products and keeping highly processed foods, fats, and vegetable oils to a minimum.

Additionally, it helps keep the natural fiber in the foods you eat. This means rather than eating white bread, choose whole-grain breads and a lot of fruits, legumes (peas, beans or lentils), and vegetables. Don't forget that physical activity is important for accomplishing and sustaining a healthy weight.

Chapter 1: Get Informed

How to get the essential nutrients that your body needs?

You can fulfill and can get all the essential nutrients that your body needs with an excellent planning and knowledge of what makes up a balanced & healthy vegan diet.

There could be chances that you miss out on vital nutrients, such as vitamin B12, calcium and iron, if you don't plan your diet properly.

Vegans who are pregnant or breastfeeding:

Women who follow a vegan diet (when breastfeeding or during pregnancy) need to ensure that they get sufficient amount of minerals and vitamins for their child to grow healthily.

You need to make sure that your child gets a wide variety of foods to get the essential vitamins and energy he or she needs for overall body growth.

Vitamin B12

To maintain a healthy blood and nervous system, your body requires sufficient amount of vitamin B12. Sources for vegans to get Vitamin B12 are very limited as Vitamin B12 is naturally found in foods from animal sources. A supplement of vitamin B12 may be looked-for.

Good sources of Vitamin B12 for vegans and vegetarians:

- Yeast extract like Marmite
- Fortified soya drinks or breakfast cereals

How to get vitamin D and calcium for your body?

For healthy and strong teeth and bones, your body needs calcium. People who don't follow vegan diet get most of their calcium need from dairy foods (such as yogurt, milk and cheese), however; vegans may get it fulfill from other foods sources as well.

Good sources of calcium for vegans include:

- Dried fruit such as dried apricots, raisins, figs & prunes
- Fortified rice, soya & oat drinks
- Tahini & sesame seeds
- Calcium-set tofu
- White and brown bread
- Pulses

To absorb calcium, your body needs vitamin D. Vegan sources of vitamin D are:

- Vitamin D supplements (to make sure that the vitamin D used in a product is not of animal origin, you may read the label)

- Fortified fat spreads, soya drinks and breakfast cereals (with added vitamin D)
- Exposure to sunlight – don't forget to protect or cover up your skin before it starts to burn or turn red

Getting enough iron

Your body requires "Iron" to make red blood cells. Your body absorbs less quantity of Iron that comes from plant-based food.

Vegans can get iron from:

- Whole meal flour and bread
- Pulses
- Dark-green leafy vegetables such as spring greens, watercress and broccoli
- Breakfast cereals fortified with iron
- Dried fruits like prunes, figs and apricots
- Nuts

How to get omega-3 fatty acids in vegan diet:

Omega-3 fatty acids primarily found in fish and when eaten as part of a healthy diet can help your body to maintain a healthy heart & decrease your chances of heart diseases.

Vegans may get omega-3 fatty acids through following sources:

- Walnuts

- Rapeseed oil
- Linseed (flaxseed) oil
- Soya-based foods like tofu and Soya oil

Chapter 2: Benefits

Few benefits that you would be getting from a vegan (Plant Based) diet:

One major weight loss benefit of a plant-based diet is satiety. Plant foods have high water content:

- Green vegetables contain 90 percent or more water
- Potatoes & root vegetables contain 70 percent or even more water
- Cooked grains can be 70% or more water
- Fresh fruits are typically more than 80% water

Vegetables like Brussels sprouts, broccoli, cabbage, cauliflower, turnips, and kale contain in them doles & flavones, which are well known to have anti-cancer elements included in them. Vitamin C normally found in a lot of vegetables and citrus fruits may actually lower the risks of stomach and esophagus cancers. Vitamin C helps blocking the conversion of nitrates to cancer-causing nitrosamines in the stomach. It also acts as an antioxidant, counteracting the cancer-causing chemicals that normally form inside your body. Selenium is generally found in whole grains and it has similar antioxidant effects like vitamin C and beta-carotene. Even Vitamin E has this effect as well. Don't supplement selenium in large doses; get in touch with your doctor about this.

A vegan or plant-based diet is your key for your overall health. You will enjoy benefits such as:

- Better sleep
- Stops afternoon fatigue
- Improve strength
- Prevent colds or the flu
- Prevent aches and pains
- Improve overall mood
- Reduce excess body fat
- Relieve joint pain
- Gain muscle.

Plant-based foods are alkalizing—keeping bones strong and healthy, while Animal-based foods are exceptionally acid forming. A plant-based diet can help manage diabetes, high blood pressure (It may also be lower in sodium and higher in potassium, which can help lower blood pressure). It may also prevent heart disease and certain cancers that scientifically generated because of foodstuffs, genetically modified foods and animal products promote. It may also help protect you from obesity, diabetes, autoimmune diseases, bones, kidneys, eyes and brain diseases.

Your skin will clear up and any acne will vanish. Plant-based meals, vegetables, and fruits are unbelievably hydrating. Your skin will glow with vibrant health. The general benefit of eating a plant-based diet is: lower in saturated fat and cholesterol, depending on your food choices.

In the subsequent of this book, I will help you with some of the breakfast, lunch, dinner, snacks and soups ideas that you can try at your home.

Chapter 3: Breakfast

Kale & Potato Hash

Total Preparation & Cooking time: 35 minutes

Serving: 4

Ingredients

- 1 shallot, medium & minced
- 1/2 large bunch torn kale leaves (approximately 8 cups)
- ½ tsp. ground pepper, fresh
- 2 cups potatoes, cooked & shredded
- 2 tbsp. horseradish
- 3 tbsp. olive oil, extra virgin
- ¼ tsp. salt

Cooking Directions

1. Put the kale leaves in a microwave-safe bowl (preferably large), cover & cook approximately 3 minutes or until wilted. Drain, let the leaves to slightly cool down, and then finely chop.

2. In the meantime, mix shallot, horseradish, salt and pepper together in a large bowl. Put in the already chopped potatoes and kale; stir to mix well.

3. Over medium heat in a large nonstick skillet, heat the olive oil. Now put the kale mixture to the skillet, spread into an even layer & cook, stirring after every 2 to 3 minutes & returning the mixture to a smooth layer, approximately 12 to 15 minutes or until the potatoes becomes crispy and turns golden brown.

Nutritional Value (Amount Per Serving): 220.4 Calories, 11.2 g Total Fat, 0 mg Cholesterol, 28 g Carbohydrate, 4.6 g Fiber, 6.1 g Protein

Delicious Scrambled Tofu

Total Preparation & Cooking time: 25 minutes

Serves: 6

Ingredients

- 2 green onions, chopped or 1 tbsp. onion powder
- 1 tbsp. soy sauce
- 1 tbsp. Italian seasoning
- 2 tbsp. green pimientos, dried (optional) or 1 tbsp. green chilies, canned (optional)
- 1 green bell pepper, chopped
- 1/4 tsp. turmeric
- 1-pound firm tofu
- 1/2 tsp. salt
- 1 to 2 tomatoes, chopped
- black salt, as per requirements

Cooking Directions

1. Use your hands to crumble the tofu.

2. Mix tofu & everything together well in a skillet (don't add the tomatoes). Heat approximately 8 to 10 minutes.

3. Now, put in the tomatoes & then heating approximately 5 to 8 more minutes or until thoroughly heated.

Nutritional Value (Amount Per Serving): 66.7 Calories, 3.2 g Total Fat, 0 mg Cholesterol, 4.2 g Carbohydrate, 1.4 g Fiber, 7 g Protein

Tropical Oatmeal

Total Preparation & Cooking time: 6 *minutes*

Serves: 1

Ingredients

- ½ banana, medium
- ½ tsp. coconut extract
- ½ cup oatmeal
- Sugar substitute such as Splenda
- 1 cup water

Cooking Directions

1. Cook oatmeal either in stovetop or in microwave as you usually do.

2. Slice up the banana approximately ¼" slices and make four pieces out of it at the same time as you are cooking.

3. When you are done with the oatmeal, add banana and coconut extract. To make thin oatmeal, you may add a small quantity of milk with a sweetener, if desired.

Nutritional Value (Amount Per Serving): 211 Calories, 2.8 g Total Fat, 0 mg Cholesterol, 40.9 g Carbohydrate, 5.6 g Fiber, 6 g Protein

Oat Waffles

Total Preparation & Cooking time: 10 *minutes*

Serves: 4 waffles

Ingredients

- 1 sliced banana
- 2 cups water
- 1 tsp. vanilla
- 2 cups rolled oats
- 1 tbsp. sugar
- 1⁄2 tsp. salt

Cooking Directions

1. Put everything in a high-speed blender & blend until smooth.

2. Transfer the paste to a cast iron waffle.

Nutritional Value (Amount Per Serving)195 Calories, 2.7 g Total Fat, 0 mg Cholesterol, 37.4 g Carbohydrate, 4.9 g Fiber, 5.6 g Protein

Rice & Raisin Pudding

Total Preparation & Cooking time: 20 *minutes*

Serves: 4

Ingredients

- 1 cup of water
- 1 cup of soy milk
- 1/2 cup of raisins
- 3 cups of cooked brown rice
- 1/4 cup of real maple syrup
- 1/2 cup od toasted and chopped almonds
- 1 tsp. ground cinnamon
- 1/2 tsp. ground cardamom

Cooking Directions

1. Start off by adding all the ingredients together.

2. Bring to a boil over medium to high heat.

3. Immediately reduce the heat to low and simmer.

4. Stir it frequently to prevent scorching. Repeat until it thickened, about 5-8 minutes.

5. Spoon into your favorite bowl and serve.

Nutritional Value (Amount Per Serving) 406 Calories, 11.6 g Total Fat, 0 mg Cholesterol, 68.9 g Carbohydrate, 6.1 g Fiber, 10.2 g Protein

Dried Fruit and Nut Granola

Total Preparation & Cooking time: 40 *minutes*

Serves: 6

Ingredients

- 2 cups rolled oats
- 1⁄2 cup packed brown sugar
- 1⁄4 cup cranberries, dried & diced
- 1 tsp. cinnamon, ground
- 1⁄4 cup orange juice
- 1⁄2 cup flour, all-purpose
- 3 tbsp. vegetable oil
- 1⁄2 tsp. ginger, ground
- 1⁄4 cup apricot, dried & diced
- 1⁄2 cup chopped nuts (or your choice)
- 3 tbsp. pure maple syrup

Cooking Directions

1. Line a baking sheet with aluminum foil and preheat the oven at 300F /175C. Spray vegetable spray over the baking sheet.

2. In a mixing bowl, mix together the flour, oats, cinnamon, sugar, oil, ginger, maple syrup, nuts and orange juice. Put the mixture over the prepared baking sheet & bake approximately half an hour, to prevent burning, you need to toss it once. Now put in the dried fruit.

3. You may store the Granola in an airtight container approximately for 1 month.

Nutritional Value (Amount Per Serving): 385.8 Calories, 14.6 g Total Fat, 0 mg Cholesterol, 58.8 g Carbohydrate, 4.8 g Fiber, 7.7 g Protein

Herb-Roasted Potatoes

Total Preparation & Cooking time: 75 *minutes*

Serves: 6

Ingredients

- 1 onion, medium & quartered ad sliced into half inch thick
- 3 pounds red potatoes, small & halved widthwise
- 4 tsp. thyme, fresh & chopped
- 3 dashes black pepper, fresh
- 4 tsp. rosemary, fresh & chopped
- 1/4 cup olive oil
- 2 tsp. coarse sea salt

Cooking Directions

1. Preheat your oven at 450F/230C.

2. Divide the onions & potatoes either between a large rimmed baking sheet or two rimmed baking pans, sprinkle oil and then pepper and salt. Toss to coat well (you may even use your hands to perform this).

3. Roast approximately half an hour and then remove the potatoes from the oven. Sprinkle herbs & toss to coat well (since potatoes must be hot, you may use a spatula) return the potatoes to the oven & roast approximately 20 more minutes or until brown and tender.

Nutritional Value (Amount Per Serving): 395 g Calories, 13.9 g Total Fat, 0 mg Cholesterol, 62.7 g Carbohydrate, 8.1 g Fiber, 7.2 g Protein

Breakfast Quinoa

Total Preparation & Cooking time: 30 *minutes*

Serves: 4

Ingredients

- 1 cup quinoa (uncooked and rinsed)
- 1 cup of water
- 1 cup apricot nectar (or other nectar, no extra sugar added)
- 1 cup of blueberries (rinsed)
- 2 apples (cored and rinsed)
- 2 cups of plain yogurt (no sugar added and nonfat)
- 2 tbsp. of chopped walnuts

Cooking Directions

1. Feel free to change up the fruit mixtures. Take the rinsed quinoa, water, and nectar to a boil. Reduce to a simmer and cover. Cook it until all the liquid is absorbed, takes about 10-15 minutes.

2. Remove it from heat and allow it to cool. Once quinoa is cool completely, toss with diced apples, chopped walnuts, and blueberries.

3. Top it with yogurt and serve.

Nutritional Value (Amount Per Serving): 371 g Calories, 6.7 g Total Fat, 7 mg Cholesterol, 63.1 g Carbohydrate, 6.7 g Fiber, 14.7 g Protein

Cherry Almond Cereal

Total Preparation & Cooking time: 5 *minutes*

Serves: 1

Ingredients

- 8 cherries, pitted & quartered
- 1/3 cup soymilk
- 1/2 banana, large & sliced into 1/2 moons
- 2 tbsp. almond butter (honey-sweetened or natural, both are good)
- 3/4-1 cup organic multigrain flakes

Cooking Directions

1. Put the flakes in a large bowl & spoon the almond butter over it. (Ensure that the almond butter is softer and easier to stir in.)

2. Now, put in the soymilk & stir everything. If you see clumps of flakes and almond butter; don't worry, this is normal.

3. Put the remaining fruits over it, and stir quickly! Serve and enjoy.

Nutritional Value (Amount Per Serving): 381.3 Calories, 16.7 g Total Fat, 0 mg Cholesterol, 56.3 g Carbohydrate, 9.9 g Fiber, 11.5 g Protein

Mighty Chickpea Pancake

Total Preparation & Cooking time: 20 *minutes*

Serves: 1 big pancake

Ingredients

- 1 finely chopped green onion (about 1/4 cup)
- 1/4 cup finely chopped red pepper
- 1/2 cup chickpea flour (also known as besan or garbanzo flour)
- 1/4 tsp. garlic power
- 1/4 tsp. baking power
- 1/4 tsp. fine grain sea salt
- 1/8 tsp. freshly ground black
- 1/2 cup and 2 tbsp. water
- pinch red pepper flacks (optional)
- avocado, hummus, cashew cream, and salsa (optional when serving)

Cooking Directions

1. Prepare the ingredients and set aside. Preheat a 10-inch skillet over medium heat.

2. Take chickpea flour, garlic power, salt, baking powder, pepper, (optional) red pepper flakes and whisk them in a small bowl.

3. Add water in the bowl. Whisk it respectively until no clumps remain. It is preferred to whisk it for about 15 seconds to create air bubbles in the batter.

4. Add in the chopped vegetables and stir.

5. Once the skillet is preheated, spray it extensively with olive oil or other non-stick cooking spray.

6. Pour in all of the batter you have and quickly spread it out all over the pan. Cook the pancake for about 5-6 minutes, depending on how hot your pan is. Then flip the pancake with caution and cook for additional 5 minutes, until it looks lightly golden. When cooking, make sure to take your time because this pancake takes much longer time to cook compared to regular pancakes.

7. Serve the dish on a large plate and top it with your choice of toppings. Leftovers can be wrapped up and stored in the fridge. Reheat on a skillet until warmed throughout.

Nutritional Value (Amount Per Serving): 381 Calories, 6.1 g Total Fat, 29 mg Cholesterol, 64.5 g Carbohydrate, 18.5 g Fiber, 20 g Protein

Chapter 4: Lunch

Dulse, Tomato & Lettuce Sandwiches

Total Preparation & Cooking time: 10 _minutes_

Serves: 2

Ingredients

- 4 slices whole-grain bread
- 4 tbsp. mayonnaise, vegan
- 1/2 cup Dulse seaweed
- 1 tomatoes
- 1/2 cup lettuce

Cooking Directions

1. Over medium heat in a large skillet, dry fry the Dulse until the leaves turn greenish, (black=burnt) for a few minutes. Let it cool at room temperature.

2. In the meantime, make the tomato slice and toast bread, if desired. Spread mayonnaise over the bread. Top the bread with Dulse, tomato, and lettuce. Season with pepper and salt, if desired.

Nutritional Value (Amount Per Serving): 224.2 Calories, 7.7 g Total Fat, 7.2 mg Cholesterol, 34.6 g Carbohydrate, 2.2 g Fiber, 5.2 g Protein

Sugar and Spice Almonds

Total Preparation & Cooking time: 15 *minutes*

Serves: 2 cups

Ingredients

- 2 cups whole almonds
- 3 tbsp. light corn syrup
- 1/3 cup granulated sugar (or vegan sugar)
- 1/2 tsp. nutmeg, freshly ground
- 4 tsp. ground cinnamon

Cooking Directions

1. Preheat your oven at 350 F/175 C.

2. Spray a baking sheet (preferably large) with cooking spray (non-sticking), or put a few drops of oil & use a paper towel to spread it evenly.

3. Combine sugar, nutmeg, and cinnamon in a small dish and keep it aside.

4. Combine the corn syrup with the almonds until the almonds are well coated in a different bowl; sprinkle sugar over the almonds and stir. Ensure it gets mixed in evenly.

5. Put the coated almonds on the greased baking sheet & bake until the almonds are browned & bubbly, approximately 15 minutes; remove the almonds from the oven.

6. Let the almonds cool down on the baking sheet at the room temperature, stirring to separate the nuts and to prevent sticking.

7. You may even store the crispy almonds in an airtight container, not for that long!

Nutritional Value (Amount Per Serving): 1063.8 Calories, 72.8 g Total Fat, 0 mg Cholesterol, 90.8 g Carbohydrate, 19.5 g Fiber, 30.6 g Protein

Roasted Green Beans

Total Preparation & Cooking time: 25 *minutes*

Serves: 6

Ingredients

- 2 pounds' green beans
- 2 tbsp. olive oil
- 1 tsp. kosher salt
- 1⁄2 tsp. ground pepper, fresh

Cooking Directions

1. Preheat your oven at 400F/200 C.

2. Wash and rinse the green beans (make sure that the beans are neat, dry well).

3. Arrange the green beans on a jelly roll pan & drizzle olive oil over it.

4. Sprinkle with pepper and salt to taste.

5. Coat the beans evenly using your hands and then spread the beans out into one layer.

6. Roast until beans are somewhat shriveled and fairly brown in the spots, approximately half an hour; don't forget to turn the beans after every 10 to 15 minutes.

7. Serve at room temperature or hot.

Nutritional Value (Amount Per Serving): 100.9 Calories, 3.9 g Total Fat, 0 mg Cholesterol, 16 g Carbohydrate, 6.2 g Fiber, 4.2 g Protein

Cauliflower Popcorn

Total Preparation & Cooking time: 70 *minutes*

Serves: 4

Ingredients

- 1 head cauliflower
- 4 tbsp. olive oil
- 1 tsp. salt, to taste

Cooking Directions

1. Preheat your oven at 425 F/220 C.

2. Trim the head of the cauliflower and discard the thick stems and core; cut the florets and make Ping-Pong balls size pieces.

3. Mix the salt and olive oil together in a large bowl, whisk and then put the cauliflower pieces & toss thoroughly.

4. For easy cleanup, line a baking sheet with parchment then spread the cauliflower pieces on the sheet & roast until most of the pieces have turned golden brown, approximately an hour, turning 4 or 5 times.

Nutritional Value (Amount Per Serving): 156.1
Calories, 13.9 g Total Fat, 0 mg Cholesterol, 7.3 g Carbohydrate, 2.9 g Fiber, 2.8 g Protein

Onions and Spinach

Total Preparation & Cooking time: 25 *minutes*

Serves: 4

Ingredients

- 3 tbsp. light olive oil
- 1 red onion, large & thinly sliced
- 1-pound spinach leaves, fresh, cleaned & stems removed
- 1 tbsp. lemon juice, fresh
- pepper and salt (as per taste)

Cooking Directions

1. Heat olive oil in a large skillet.

2. Add onions, only when the oil gets hot, ensure it's not smoking.

3. Sauté, until the onion is caramelized, stirring constantly, approximately 15 min let some of the onion get crisp and quite dark.

4. Now put the spinach leaves, for a minute or two & stir until just wilted.

5. Now put in the lemon juice, pepper & salt and mix with the prepared dish.

6. Serve.

Nutritional Value (Amount Per Serving):131.4
Calories, 10.6 g Total Fat, 0 mg Cholesterol
7.9 g Carbohydrate, 3.2 g Fiber, 3.7 g Protein

Roasted Garlic & Broccoli

Total Preparation & Cooking time: 35 *minutes*

Serves: 6

Ingredients

- 9 cups broccoli florets
- 12 oz. garlic, peeled & cloves separated (approximately 3 heads)
- 2 tbsp. soy sauce
- 1 tsp. sesame oil
- 2 tsp. olive oil

Cooking Directions

1. Lightly oil a baking pan (preferably 8-10" square).

2. Put olive oil in the pan & mix with the garlic cloves.

3. Bake at 475F /245C approximately 20 minutes; until the garlic starts becoming brown (don't overdo it).

4. Bring a pot (preferably large) of water to boil, while the garlic is still roasting.

5. Add the broccoli to the water, the moment it starts boiling & cook approximately 5 minutes (just heat the broccoli and ensure it's still very crisp).

6. Drain and then put it in cold water. Drain and repeat the process with broccoli.

7. Mix the sesame oil & soy sauce in a shallow bowl and then add the mixture to the garlic & stir.

8. Put this mixture over the broccoli & toss well.

Nutritional Value (Amount Per Serving): 98 Calories, 2.8 g Total Fat, 0 mg Cholesterol, l15.8 g Carbohydrate, 0.7 g Fiber, 5.7 g Protein

Candied Peanuts

Total Preparation & Cooking time: 15 *minutes*

Serves: 4

Ingredients

- 2 cups peanuts, roasted & unsalted
- 1 tsp. lemon juice
- 1 cup sugar

Cooking Directions

o   Over medium heat in a saucepan, melt the sugar completely, stirring frequently.

1   Add lemon juice to the sugar only when the sugar reaches the consistency of corn syrup, stirring quickly.

2   Remove the mixture from the heat & stir in the peanuts quickly. To make the coated peanuts hard, spread them on an oiled baking sheet.

Nutritional Value (Amount Per Serving): 580.1 Calories, 32.8 g Total Fat, 0 mg Cholesterol, 62.7 g Carbohydrate, 4.6 g Fiber, 17.5 g Protein

Asian Vegan Salad

Total Preparation & Cooking time: 20 *minutes*

Serves: 4

Ingredients

Salad

- 1 bunch kale (Any type of your choice, but preferably lacinato/Tuscan/dinosaur kale)
- fine-grain sea salt
- 1 cup of chopped snow peas
- 1 large carrot (peeled and ribboned)
- 1 small red bell pepper (seeded and chopped)
- 1 heaping cup of organic edamame
- a avocado (pitted and sliced into small chucks)
- 1 large shallot (nicely sliced)
- handful of cilantro (chopped)
- handful of Thai basil or regular basil (chopped)

Sauce

- 1/4 cup olive oil
- 2 tbsp. rice vinegar
- 1 tbsp. finely grated ginger
- 1 tbsp. low-sodium tamari (or other low-sodium soy sauce)
- 2 tsp. of lime juice
- 3 garlic cloves (pressed or minced)

Cooking Directions

1. With a chef's knife, remove the tough ribs from the kale, then discard them. Chop the kale leaves into bite-size pieces and transfer them to a bowl.

2. Sprinkle the kale leaves with a dash of sea salt and massage the kale leaves with your hands until the kale is darker green and fragrant.

3. Place the remaining salad dressing with the kale and toss to coat well.

4. Start to make the vinaigrette: whisk together all the ingredients until emulsified. Toss the dressing with the kale salad and serve.

Nutritional Value (Amount Per Serving): 365 Calories, 27 g Total Fat, 0 mg Cholesterol, 23.2 g Carbohydrate, 8.6 g Fiber, 12 g Protein

Cabbage & Caraway Combo

Total Preparation & Cooking time: 20 *minutes*

Serves: 4

Ingredients

- 1 savoy cabbage (cored and shredded)
- 1 tbsp. olive oil
- 1 onion (thinly sliced)
- 2 or 3 tsp. caraway seeds

Cooking Directions

1. Cook the cabbage in boiling water until tender, about 3 minutes, then drain.

2. Heat a frying pan and add the oil. Now add the onion and cook until they are soft and turn golden, about 2-3 minutes.

3. Sprinkle over the caraway seeds and cook until fragrant, about 2 minutes.

4. Add the cabbage, stir and heat through.

Nutritional Value (Amount Per Serving): 98 Calories, 4 g Total Fat, 0 mg Cholesterol, 11g Carbohydrate, 7 g Fiber, 5 g Protein

Big Vegan Bowl

Total Preparation & Cooking time: 55 *minutes*

Serves: 2 big bowls

Ingredients

- 1 large sweet potato (chopped into 3/4 inch cubes)
- 1 can of chickpeas (15-ounce), drained and rinsed (about 1.5 cups)
- 1 cup uncooked quinoa
- 1 large carrot (peeled and julienned)
- hummus (more is preferred)
- a handful of greens for the base (optional)
- purple cabbage or vegetable of choice (shredded)
- sliced avocado
- hulled hemp seeds

Cooking Directions

1. Preheat the oven to 400 F. Arrange two large baking sheet with parchment paper.

2. Have the chopped sweet potato spread out on one sheet. Pour 1/2 teaspoon of oil on the sweet potatoes. Then toast it until it is coated. Next use grain sea salt and sprinkle them on the sweet potatoes.

3. Drain and wash the chickpeas. Place them on a large tea towel. Pat it until it becomes completely dry. Remove any skins that comes off. Then, move the chickpeas to the

baking sheet. Use 1/2 teaspoon oil and spread on it. Rub them around with your hands until lightly coated. Lightly sprinkle with fine grain sea salt and your favorite spices. (Personal Recommendation) use garlic powder, chili powder, cumin, cayenne, and salt. Toss gently to combine.

4. Insert both the chickpeas and the sweet potato into the preheated oven. Set it to 400 F and remove them after roast for 15 minutes. Flip the sweet potatoes and and softly roll around the chickpeas. Then, put them back into the oven for another 15 minutes. (Be cautious at the last 5 minutes). When the chickpeas are golden and the sweet potatoes are light brown on the bottom and fork tender, they are ready to be taken out from the oven.

5. While roasting, cook the quinoa. Rinse the quinoa in a fine mesh sieve and place it in a medium pot. Add 1 and a half cup of water and stir it. Set the mixture to a low boil. Then reduce the heat to medium/low and cover the lid. Simmer it for about 14-17 minutes (you can check back on it after 13 minutes), until all the water is fully absorbed and the quinoa is fluffy. Remove the heat and leave the lid onto the steam for an extra 5-10 minutes or longer if necessary. Fluff it with fork.

6. To assemble the bowl: Add a few handful amount of greens into a large bowl. When the roasted chickpeas and veggies are completely, allow the chickpeas to cool down for 5 minutes. Then add them on the salad followed by the sliced hummus, hemp seeds, sliced avocado and

shredded veggies. Plate each of them by sections: One for veggies and etc.

7. Serve and enjoy! If you prefer to use dressing, you can.

Nutritional Value (Amount Per Serving): 1388 Calories, 37.8 g Total Fat, 0 mg Cholesterol, 214.3 g Carbohydrate, 53.6 g Fiber, 57.1 g Protein

Chapter 5: Dinner

Cheese Pasta

Total Preparation & Cooking time: 15 *minutes*

Serves: 3

Ingredients

- macaroni noodles or tortilla chips
- 1⁄4 cup nutritional yeast flakes
- 1 can tomatoes, diced with green chilies
- 1⁄4 cup flour
- 1 -2 tbsp. mayonnaise, vegan
- 1⁄4-1⁄2 tsp. pepper
- paprika
- cayenne pepper
- 1 cup water

Cooking Directions

1. Sift the dry ingredients together in a medium saucepan.

2. Over medium heat, whisk the ingredients in water until bubbly.

3. Stir in tomatoes and margarine.

4. Continue cooking until well heated.

5. You may serve this over noodles for Mac & cheese, or over chips for nachos.

Nutritional Value (Amount Per Serving): 99.7 Calories, 0.9 g Total Fat, 0 mg Cholesterol, 17.6 g Carbohydrate, 3.7 g Fiber, 7.9 g Protein

Spicy Veggie Salad

Total Preparation & Cooking time: 30 *minutes*

Serves: 6

Ingredients

*   3 chopped tomatoes
*   2 cups corn kernels (frozen or fresh)
*   1/2 cup chopped cilantro, fresh
*   2 diced celery ribs
*   1 green bell pepper, sliced
*   3 sliced onions, green
*   2 avocados, ripe & chopped
*   1 cup sprouted lentils

Dressing

*   1/2 tsp. ground cumin
*   2 tbsp. olive oil, extra-virgin
*   1 tbsp. flax seed oil
*   2 cloves garlic, minced
*   1-1 1/2 limes juice, fresh
*   1 tbsp. agave nectar
*   1 tsp. chili, fresh & minced
*   tbsp. tamari

Cooking Directions

1. Mix the dressing ingredients first and keep them aside for sometime so that they can get the desired flavors.

2. Now, in a large bowl, mix the salad ingredients together.

3. Mix the dressing ingredients with the salad ingredients and toss well.

Nutritional Value (Amount Per Serving): 536.2 Calories, 0.2 mg Cholesterol, 552.6 mg Sodium, 70.3 g Carbohydrate, 17.7 g Fiber, 5.9 g Sugars, 15.9 g Protein

Fried Tofu

Total Preparation & Cooking time: 20 *minutes*

Serves: 3

Ingredients

- 1 tbsp. soya sauce or 3 tbsp. tamari
- 1 package extra firm tofu (approximately 350 grams)
- 1 tsp. seasoning
- 1 tbsp. olive oil
- ¼ cup Red Star nutritional yeast

Cooking Directions

1. Put few drops of oil on a non-stick pan.

2. Put soy sauce (tamari) in a bowl.

3. Mix spices & yeast in another bowl.

4. Slice the tofu into ¼" slices.

5. First dip tofu in soy sauce & then in yeast mixture.

6. Fry the tofu until it becomes golden; brown the other side.

7. You may add a small quantity of oil, if required.

Nutritional Value (Amount Per Serving): 198.4 Calories, 14.1 g Total Fat, 0 mg Cholesterol, 4.5 g Carbohydrate, 1.8 g Fiber, 17.2 g Protein

Fried Rice

Total Preparation & Cooking time: 20 *minutes*

Serves: 4

Ingredients

- 2 cups cooked rice, leftover
- oil
- 1 diced onion
- 2 tsp. garlic, minced
- 2 cups mixed vegetables, frozen
- 3 cups bean sprouts, loosely packed
- ½ tsp. turmeric
- 1 tbsp. light soy sauce
- 1 cup button mushroom, sliced

Cooking Directions

1. In a large pan, heat oil over medium heat.

2. Sauté garlic and onions till limp.

3. Put in the frozen vegetables and mushrooms.

4. Cook till vegetables have warmed through and are no longer cold.

5. Add turmeric to the vegetables and mix well.

6. Now add the leftover rice & toss well. Break up any clumps.

7. Add the soy sauce in & toss, ensure that it's mixed well.

8. Serve hot.

Nutritional Value (Amount Per Serving): 438.4 Calories, 1.4 g Total Fat, 0 mg Cholesterol, 92.4 g Carbohydrate, 7.6 g Fiber, 16.4 g Protein

Spicy Chickpeas

Total Preparation & Cooking time: 30 *minutes*

Serves: 6

Ingredients

For Chickpeas

- 2 cups onions, finely chopped
- 1/4 cup cilantro, fresh & chopped
- 2 cans chickpeas, rinsed & drained (approximately 15 oz.)
- 1 tsp. lemon juice, fresh
- 1/4 cup oil
- 1 tsp. black pepper
- 3/4 tsp. salt

For Garam Masala

- 1/4 tsp. cayenne pepper
- 1 tsp. ground cumin
- 2 tsp. ground coriander
- 1/4 tsp. ground turmeric

Cooking Directions

1. Mix all the spices until well blended to make the masala and keep it aside.

2. Over med-high heat, heat the oil. Add onions & sauté approximately 10 minutes, until light brown. Now put the masala on the onions; stir until spices are fragrant, approximately a minute.

3. Stir in the chickpeas, salt, pepper and one tablespoon of water. Cook over medium heat until the first few chickpeas start to split, approximately 10 minutes, stirring constantly. Add some more (only one tablespoon at time) water, if it becomes dry. Chickpeas must be moist and not saucy.

4. Remove the chickpeas from the heat. Stir in the lemon juice & garnish it with fresh cilantro.

Nutritional Value (Amount Per Serving): 275.3 Calories, 11 g Total Fat, 0 mg Cholesterol, 38 g Carbohydrate, 7.6 g Fiber, 7.8 g Protein

Delicious Vegan Rice

Total Preparation & Cooking time: 25 *minutes*

Serves: 4

Ingredients

- ½ mushroom
- ½ white onion
- 2 cups rice
- 1 Maggie vegetable bouillon cube
- ½ cup bell pepper (red and green)
- 1 Serrano pepper
- ¼ tsp. cumin (Jeera powder)
- ½ cup corn, beans, peas and carrots (frozen)
- 1 tsp. taco seasoning
- 1 tsp. oil

Cooking Directions

1. Dice all the vegetables, except the mushroom it should be diced in bigger pieces.

2. Cook the rice & set aside.

3. Heat oil; add Serrano pepper and onion, sauté till lightly brown.

4. Now put in cumin and sauté again until lightly golden.

5. Put the veggies and the bouillon cube in but don't add the water.

6. Cook until veggies are completely cooked.

7. Sprinkle salt over the veggies.

8. Add the cooked rice and mix well.

9. Lightly sprinkle the taco seasoning and mix.

Nutritional Value (Amount Per Serving): 371.9 Calories, 1.8 g Total Fat, 0 mg Cholesterol, 79.8 g Carbohydrate, 2 g Fiber, 6.8 g Protein

Vegetarian Tacos

Total Preparation & Cooking time: 20 *minutes*

Serves: 6

Ingredients

- 2 can garbanzo beans (approximately 15 oz.)
- 1 packet taco seasoning (approximately 1 1/4 oz.)
- hard taco shells or 10 tortillas

Cooking Directions

1. Reserve the liquid of first can and then drain the garbanzo beans. Use cold running water to rinse the beans in a strainer.

2. Put the reserved bean liquid and the beans to a skillet (preferably large).

3. Put in the taco seasoning.

4. Stir & allow it to simmer approximately 15 minutes. If desired, to thicken the mixture, you may mash ¼ to 1/3 of beans while cooking.

5. Use garbanzos similarly like taco meat. Try taco shells and make a friendly taco salad or pile it high with tomato, lettuce, cheese, and salsa.

Nutritional Value (Amount Per Serving): 815.7 Calories, 16 g Total Fat, 0 mg Cholesterol, 142.9 g Carbohydrate, 16.4 g Fiber, 25 g Protein

Quinoa Bowls

Total Preparation & Cooking time: 20 *minutes*

Serves: 5

Ingredients

- 1/2 cup quinoa
- 1 tbsp. olive oil
- 1 small red bell pepper (seeded and diced)
- 1 small broccoli crown (broken into florets)
- 2 tbsp. peanut butter
- 1 tbsp. fresh lime juice
- 1 tbsp. water
- 1 tsp. tamari (or soy sauce)
- 1/2 tsp. brown sugar (or coconut sugar)
- 1/2 tsp. freshly grated ginger
- 4 slices baked tofu
- 2 tbsp. chopped roasted peanuts
- salt and pepper

Cooking Directions

1. Cook the quinoa according to package directions in water or vegetable broth.

2. While the quinoa is cooking, place a medium skillet over medium-high heat and heat the olive oil.

3. Add the red pepper and cook until softened, about 3 minutes. Transfer to a large bowl.

4. Now add the broccoli to the skillet with 2 tablespoons of water. Cover the skillet and steam until the broccoli is tender, about 2 minutes. Place the broccoli to the bowl with the pepper.

5. In a small bowl, whisk the peanut butter, water, lime juice, tamari, sugar and ginger.

6. When the quinoa is ready, transfer it to the bowl with the veggies, mix everything with the peanut sauce. Season it with salt and pepper to taste.

7. Divide the quinoa-vegetable meal into 2 bowls, then top each with 1 tablespoon of chopped peanuts and 2 slices of tofu.

Nutritional Value (Amount Per Serving): 197 Calories, 11.6 g Total Fat, 0 mg Cholesterol, 15.2 g Carbohydrate, 2.8 g Fiber, 10.5 g Protein

Asian Sweet/Spicy Tofu

Total Preparation & Cooking time: 10 *minutes*

Serves: 2

Ingredients

- 7 ounces of tofu (extra firm)
- 1 tbsp. olive oil
- 1 clove garlic (minced)
- 3 cups assorted stir-fry vegetables
- 3 tbsp. sweet chili sauce
- 2 tbsp. Sriracha hot sauce
- 2 tsp. soy sauce
- few drops of fish sauce (optional)
- 2/3 cup of cooked brown rice

Cooking Directions

1. An hour before start cooking, wrap the tofu in paper towels and place between two plates to press out the liquid. Change the paper towels once during the pressing. Slice the tofu into even cubes.

2. Place a non-stick pan over medium-high heat, add the oil. Once the oil is hot, add the tofu cubes and pan fry them until golden on one side. Use tongs to turn the pieces and brown at least 4 sides of the cubes for the best texture.

3. Transfer the tofu cubes to a bowl, and if needed add some cooking spray to the pan.

4. Sauté the vegetables and garlic over medium-high heat with a bit of salt.

5. While the vegetables and tofu are cooking, stir together the sauce ingredients.

6. Serve the vegetables and tofu with the sauce over brown rice.

Nutritional Value (Amount Per Serving): 474 Calories, 12.8 g Total Fat, 0 mg Cholesterol, 72.8 g Carbohydrate, 1 g Fiber, 15.6 g Protein

Quinoa C Edamame Salad

Total Preparation & Cooking time: 145 *minutes*

Serves: 4

Ingredients

- 2 cups frozen shelled edamame
- 1 cup frozen corn
- 1 cup quinoa (cooked and cool)
- 1 green onion (sliced and green parts only)
- 1/2 red sweet bell pepper (diced)
- 1.5 tbsp. olive oil
- 1 tbsp. fresh lemon juice
- 1 tbsp. fresh lime juice
- 1/4 tsp salt
- 1/4 tsp chili powder
- 1/4 tsp dried thyme
- 1/8 tsp fresh ground black pepper
- dash of cayenne

Cooking Directions

1. Briefly boil the corn and edamame, just until tender. Drain them and cool completely.

2. In a large bowl, combine the corn, edamame, quinoa, red pepper, green onion and cilantro.

3. In a small bowl, whisk together the lemon juice, lime juice, olive oil, chili pepper, black pepper, thyme, cayenne and salt until emulsified. Drizzle the mixture over salad mixture, toss to coat well.

4. Cover the bowl and chill for at least 2 hours.

Nutritional Value (Amount Per Serving): 428 Calories, 16.9 g Total Fat, 0 mg Cholesterol, 50.3 g Carbohydrate, 9.8 g Fiber, 23.9 g Protein

Conclusion/Bonus

Thank you for downloading this book!

I hope this book have provided you with the necessary knowledge to better your Vegan lifestyle.

Finally, if you enjoyed this book, then I'd like to ask you for a favor, would you be kind enough to leave a review for this book on Amazon? It'd be greatly appreciated! Even if you think this book can use some improvements please let me know and I will take action upon it.

Type in the URL below to leave a review for this book on Amazon!

http://amzn.to/1nKYfGV

Thank you and Happy Eating

But Wait There is More!

In order to show my sincere gratitude for you to choose my book to help you on your Vegan Journey I am giving you a Free book.

By going to the link below you can download another book for FREE

http://bit.ly/1PoKUe4

Printed in Great Britain
by Amazon